101 BEST CHEERS

How To
Be The Best
Cheerleader Ever!

Thanks to the Newport High School Cheerleading Squad
and Danielle Van Laeys

Published by Troll Communications, L. L. C.

101 Best Cheers is produced by becker&mayer!, Bellevue, Washington.
www.beckermayer.com
Edited by Sonja Krefting
Designed by Andrew Hess
Production management by Barbara Galvani

Printed in China

ISBN: 0-8167-7204-5
10 9 8 7 6 5 4 3

CONTENTS

INTRODUCTION

What do good sportsmanship, presentation, representation, and motivation lead to? Cheerleading!!! Cheerleading is everywhere. At the dawn of the twenty-first century, cheerleading is respected internationally as a sport and as a means of leadership in the community. Whether at a pep rally, sporting event, or fundraiser, spirited fans are supporting their schools more than ever. Cheerleaders, likewise, have become a very important part of school spirit.

Cheerleading may seem like a modern sport, but its history goes back further than you think. Cheerleading began in Great Britain during the 1860s, and soon spread to the United States. The first pep club was formed at Princeton University in 1865. Then in 1898, universities and colleges began to recognize organized cheerleading. That year, the University of Minnesota's football team was having a terrible season. The fans were so upset that one of their very own medical students, Johnny Campbell, stepped out and became the first-ever cheerleader. He stood in front of the fans and yelled: "Rah, Rah, Rah! Ski-u-mah, Hoo-rah! Hoo-rah! Varsity! Varsity! Minn-e-so-tah!" Eventually, the crowd began to catch on and supported Johnny by repeating the cheer until the entire stadium was chanting in unison. From this humble beginning, cheerleading flourished throughout the United States. At first, almost all cheerleaders were men. But when those same men were called to fight in World War II, cheerleading changed forever. Before long, more than 90% of cheerleaders were female.

Cheerleading is a lot more than pumping up the crowd and getting fans to yell cheers. Always in the spotlight, cheerleaders can be positive role models in the community. In addition to performing and cheering at games, they make signs, decorate locker rooms, organize fundraisers, and often do community service work. Football and basketball players often mention how much it helps to have cheerleaders rooting them on during grueling and difficult games. Fans also look to cheerleaders for direction and encouragement. This is where good sportsmanship comes into play. Good sportsmanship means showing a positive attitude during the good *and* bad times of a game.

In this book, you will see some of the basic moves for cheerleading along with many cheers. You can put these moves together in a way that makes sense with the words and rhythm of each cheer. You will find cheers for football, basketball, and soccer, as well as fun, general cheers to liven up any event. These cheers are set up so that you can insert your own team's name into them—simply use your team to replace the team name that is given as an example. Some cheers are meant to be performed by the cheerleading squad only, while others (called "Crowd Cheers") have places for the crowd to join in. Do not plan to become a cheerleader overnight. It takes a long time and lots of practice to become a cheerleader. Enjoy and happy cheerleading!!

This book was created by the cheerleading squad at Newport High School in Bellevue, Washington. These girls started cheering at a young age, and many of them are also dancers or gymnasts. What they all have in common, however, is hard work and dedication. These girls are:

Trudy Baidoo	Heidi Issacson	Brooke Barrus
Kasi Jones	Julia Burwell	Lea Lo
Tricia Chikuma	Sarah Short	Tamara Diles
Staci Warum	Nina Hajian	Sarah Heilman
McKenzie Holly	And our little assistant, Rachel Keylin	

Suzi J. Golden,
Newport High School Cheerleading Coach

CHEERRIFIC TIPS

★ Cheerleading is a team sport. Make sure you include everyone in all your plans. Make decisions as a group, taking everyone's ideas into account. Listen to each other carefully—everyone has something to contribute!

★ Take turns making up routines and cheers, as well as picking music.

★ If you're just starting out, learn the shorter, simpler cheers first. Once you memorize them, you can move on to longer ones.

★ Don't get hung up on the same old cheers, or you'll get tired of them. Experiment with new cheers in this book, and make up some of your own.

★ Always keep an eye out for new moves and jumps. When you learn something new, share it with your squad.

★ Take turns sitting out to watch. When you watch, you can tell your teammates what looks good, and what they need to work on. This way, everyone can improve.

★ When doing cheers, use your peripheral vision to watch your teammates. If you all keep an eye on each other, you'll stay in sync.

★ When cheering, use a loud, clear voice but do not scream. Cheer with a low-pitched as opposed to a high-pitched voice, so your words will be more easily understood. Pronounce all of the consonant sounds (such as "d," "t," and "p") especially clearly.

★ Set a steady, regular tempo for each cheer. Try not to speed up or slow down.

★ If you want the crowd to join in your cheer, let them know it's "their turn" by using motions and gestures.

★ Sometimes it can be helpful to teach a cheer to the crowd before you do it. If the crowd knows the cheer, they will be more likely to participate.

★ Keep your movements sharp and clear. Always point your toes and keep your legs straight.

★ Cheering is hard work because it combines motions and words. Take a short break between each cheer to catch your breath.

★ Always drink lots of water.

★ Always stretch before and after you cheer.

★ Do the best you can do, and don't compare yourself to other people. Some things will come more naturally to you than others. Everyone has his or her own special strengths and weaknesses. As long as you have patience, you can improve your skills all around!

ON YOUR MARK,
GET SET,
CHEER!

I'm sure you've heard it a million times—every time you play a sport or go to gym class, someone tells you to stretch, stretch, stretch! Warm-ups and stretching may seem boring, but you can't work out safely without them. Also, how can you expect to do those high kicks, exciting jumps, and mind-boggling splits without flexibility? If you stretch every day, you'll be surprised at how limber you become. Here are some important things to do before each practice or work out.

1. SCORE SOME POINTS—WARM UP YOUR JOINTS!

The joints in your wrists and ankles are delicate, and one way to avoid straining and spraining is to warm them up thoroughly. Rotate both your wrists slowly ten times in one direction, then ten times in the other direction. Then sit down on the ground and do the same thing with your ankles. This may be easier with your shoes off, because it can be hard to get a good foot stretch in stiff sneakers!

2. DON'T MOPE—JUMP ROPE!

Jumping rope is a great way to get your heart pumping, and it also builds leg muscles. Time yourself, and see how long you can jump without stopping. Try jumping with both feet, and then one at a time. Once you get better, you can experiment with some jump-roping tricks to spice things up! If you are practicing with friends, have them hold both ends of the rope as you jump, and work on your team coordination.

3. JUMPING JACK FLASH

If jumping rope isn't your style, you can try jumping jacks instead. Do your jumping jacks to music to make them more fun. Just clap your hands over your head to the beat, as you open and close your legs. Count to fifty, then take a break and do it again!

4. TRICKY TOE TOUCHES

Stand with your feet together and your arms overhead. Bend all the way over and touch your toes, with a slight bend in your knees. Hold this pose while you count to thirty, and then do it again. If you do this every day, soon you'll be able to put your hands flat on the floor.

5. A PICKY PIKE STRETCH

Sit on the floor with your legs together and straight out in front of you. Keep a slight bend in your knees. Point your toes. Reach over and try to touch your toes, keeping your head down by your knees. Now slowly (yes, even slower) count to thirty while you hold that pose. Take a little break and do it again, this time with your feet flexed. This is called a pike position, and you will see it again when you learn the pike jump.

6. A STICKLER FOR STRADDLES

Sit on the floor with your legs outstretched to either side. Keep your toes pointed and a slight bend in your knees. You are now in a straddle position—which is also a very important position for jumps. While in your straddle, stretch over one leg and see if you can kiss your knee! Then hold that pose while you count to thirty. When you're done, try the same thing on the other leg. After this, stretch out in the center between both legs, and see if you can touch your elbows to the floor. This is called a pancake stretch, but let's hold the syrup!

7. A KICK IN THE PANTS

Dancers, gymnasts, and cheerleaders are all known for kicking their legs high into the sky. Cheerleaders should do at least twenty kicks on each leg before every practice. Start with one leg behind you and your arms out to the sides for balance. Brush your leg out in front, as high as you can without hurting yourself. If your legs bend or your chest lowers, don't kick quite so high. You can practice in front of a mirror to make sure everything is straight. And remember, a good kick comes from good momentum (the way you swing your leg), not muscles.

8. THE HIPPEST HAND STANDS

If you're a gymnast, then you know the world looks better when you're upside-down. Make sure you have a padded, flat surface before you do any handstands. Don't expect to go all the way upside-down at first. Try taking a little weight in your hands at a time, until you get used to the feeling of having your hips over your head. Then you can start bringing your legs up as well. If you need help balancing, try these with your shoulders up against a wall.

9. COOLER THAN CARTWHEELS

Cartwheels are a delicate business, and you'll want to start slow. Just like the handstands, don't try to go all the way upside-down at first. You'll want to understand the pattern of your legs and arms first. Put a piece of masking tape (at least five feet long) on the floor to act as a guide. Your hands and feet should land right along this line. As you test out a cartwheel, say this to yourself: "hand, hand, foot, foot." Once you get this pattern down, you can bring your legs farther overhead.

CHEERLEADING MOVES

Here are the standard cheerleading moves most squads use in their cheers and routines. See if you can put these moves together with the cheers in this book.

T

dont

Half T

You've

been

Go Motion

Broken Arm T

know

Double Daggers

what

High V

toad,

Hip High V

Bears

Low V

Las An

Animas

Left Diagonal

Right Diagonal

as

gold

Left K

Right K

is

good

Left L

Right L

our

team

Level L (left)

Level L (right)

is

Candlesticks

the

Hands on Hips

cheer

Point Down

loudest

Low Down

 best

 we

High X

Low X

 than

the

Lunge

Blade Walk

Touchdown   Liberty

FAMOUS
CHEERLEADERS

★   Dwight D. Eisenhower   ★
★   Ronald Reagan   ★
★   Meryl Streep   ★
★   Jimmy Stewart   ★
★   Samuel L. Jackson   ★
★   Kirk Douglas   ★
★   Raquel Welch   ★
★   Teri Hatcher   ★
★   Mary McDonnell   ★
★   Reba McEntire   ★
★   Cybill Sheppard   ★

JUMP LIKE A CHAMP!

Here are some tips to help you work on jumps. It takes practice, coordination, and strong muscles to jump high in the air, but once you try it you'll see how fun it is! If you have a trampoline or a mini-tramp at home, that can be a great way to get started. If not, make sure you really use your arms in all of your jumps—you can't get off the ground without them! In addition, be careful to bend your knees deeply on take-offs and landings. This will keep you from hurting your knees, and it will give you a smooth landing every time.

PARTS OF THE JUMP

1. PREPARATION

Most cheerleading jumps start with your feet together and your weight on the balls of your feet. Begin with your arms in a high-V position so that you can get a good swing with your arms as you bend your legs. The high-V will also make your preparation look sharp and clear.

2. LIFT

If you want to jump high, timing is everything! Make sure your arms and your legs push off at exactly the same moment. As soon as your arms reach the top of their swing, your feet should be coming off the ground. Keep your body upright and look straight ahead. If you look down at the ground, guess where you'll be going next!

3. SNAPSHOT

This part is called the snapshot because you want to stay in the air long enough for someone to take your picture! When you hit the shape at the top of your jump, try to hold it for just a split second before landing! Keep your chest up, chin up, and smile!

4. LANDING

Snap your feet together quickly so you land in exactly the same position where you started. Once again, be sure to bend your knees—or you'll wake up sore in the morning!

JUMPS

These are some standard jumps you'll see in cheerleading routines and tryouts. When you learn these jumps, you can start to use them in your own cheers and choreography. Try adding at least one big jump to each of the cheers in this book!

STAG JUMP

1. Begin with your feet together and your arms by your sides.
2. With one smooth motion, hit a High V with your arms as you rise onto your toes.
3. Circle your arms in front of you and bend your legs, getting ready for your jump.
4. Jump off the ground as high as you can. Hit a High V position with your arms while you bend one leg in front and the other behind. Both legs should be turned out. Remember to keep your toes pointed.
5. Land with your feet together and arms at your sides.

STAR JUMP

1. Start with your feet together and your arms by your sides.
2. With one smooth motion, hit a High V with your arms as you rise onto your toes.
3. Circle your arms in front of your body as you bend your knees.
4. Jump up as high as you can. Hit your arms in a high V motion, and kick your legs outwards to the side, so your body forms an X or "star" shape.
5. Land with your feet together and your arms by your side.

HURDLER JUMP

1. Start with your feet together and your arms by your sides.
2. With one smooth motion, hit a High V with your arms as you rise onto your toes.
3. Circle your arms in front of your body as you bend your knees.
4. When you jump, kick one leg forward and level to your waist. Bend the other leg behind and to the side. The idea is to look like a hurdler in track. Your arms can be in a high V, or reaching toward your front foot.
5. Land with your feet together and your arms by your side.

TOE TOUCH

This is one of the most difficult jumps in cheerleading, but it also looks the coolest! This is a good one to try out on a trampoline first.

1. Begin with your feet together and your arms by your sides.
2. With one smooth motion, hit a High V with your arms as you rise onto your toes.
3. Circle your arms in front of your body as you bend your legs.
4. Jump off the ground as high as you can. Kick your feet out to the side, and reach for your toes. Your hands will probably only reach as far as your ankles, but that will still be impressive! Be sure to keep your chest up as you hit your pose.
5. Land with your feet together and your arms by your side.

GENERAL CHEERS

KEY

(YELL)	=	Spoken by the crowd
BEARS	=	Your Team Name
🖐	=	Clap
👞	=	Stomp

POWER, STRENGTH, MIGHT

POWER, STRENGTH, MIGHT
WE WILL WIN THIS GAME TONIGHT
OUR SPIRITS ARE HIGH
OUR TEAM IS SUPER HOT
THE *NORTH FOREST TIGERS*
    WILL ROCK YOU TO THE TOP
THE CLOCK IS TICKING
THE GAME WILL SOON BE DONE
POWER, STRENGTH, MIGHT,
MAKE US NUMBER ONE TONIGHT!

CLAP YOUR HANDS

CLAP YOUR HANDS, STOMP YOUR FEET
AND LISTEN TO THE RHYTHM OF THE
    COMETS' BEAT!

GENERATE

GENERATE SOME SPIRIT
GENERATE SOME HEAT
YOU'VE GOT TO GET THE BEAT
UH-HUH, GET THE BEAT!

DIG IT!

D-I-G I DIG IT!
DRAGONS FANS, WE LOVE IT
DRAGONS FANS, CAN'T STOP IT
STRAIGHT TO THE TOP, LET'S ROCK IT!

GOT THE POWER

TIGERS GOT THE POWER
TIGERS GOT THE POWER
TIGERS GOT THE POWER
    TO MAKE YOU SHAKE SOMETHIN'
TIGERS GOT THE POWER
TIGERS GOT THE POWER
TIGERS GOT THE POWER
    TO MAKE YOU ROLL SOMETHIN'
TIGERS GOT THE POWER
TIGERS GOT THE POWER
TIGERS GOT THE POWER
    TO MAKE YOU GET DOWN!

LISTEN TO THE SOUND

LISTEN TO THE SOUND,
    TO THE SOUND OF THE BEAT
LISTEN TO THE SOUND,
    TO THE SOUND OF OUR FEET
IT GOES, 👞 👏 👞 👞 👞 👏 [repeat three times]
GO, FIGHT, WIN!

CLAP

CLAP YOUR HANDS EVERYBODY 👏
EVERYBODY CLAP YOUR HANDS 👏
CAUSE WE ARE THE *RANGERS*,
THE BEST IN THE LAND!

ROLLIN' IN STYLE

WE, THE *BRONCOS*
ARE ROLLIN' IN STYLE
AND IF YOU THINK YOUR HEART CAN'T
 TAKE IT
COME AND ROLL A WHILE
ROLL A WHILE!

GET YOURSELVES TOGETHER

GET YOURSELVES TOGETHER, *HAWKS*
GET YOURSELVES TOGETHER
AND SCORE SOME POINTS!

REACHING FOR THE TOP

ARE YOU READY TO BE CHALLENGED?
ARE YOU READY TO BE STOPPED?
WE'RE THE MIGHTY *PIONEERS*
AND WE'RE REACHING FOR THE TOP!

MOVE IT

MOVE IT, DOWN THE FIELD
GO THAT WAY! 👏 👏 👏

WE GOT SPIRIT

WE GOT SPIRIT
UH-HUH, WHAT?
WE GOT SPIRIT
UH-HUH, WHAT?
WE GOT
NORTH, SOUTH, EAST, WEST
THE *ROYALS* ARE THE BEST!

WHAT

WE'VE GOT SPIRIT
YEAH, YEAH
WE'VE GOT SPIRIT
YEAH, YEAH
WE'VE GOT WHAT, WHAT, WHAT, WHAT [slow]
WHAT, WHAT, WHAT, WHAT, WHAT, WHAT,
    WHAT [fast]
WE'VE GOT SPIRIT!

L-E-T-S G-O

L-E-T-S G-O
LET'S GO, LET'S GO
L-E-T-S G-O
BROWNS, LET'S GO!

"Cheerleading is great when everyone works together. Keep an open mind and take criticism in a positive manner."
—Tricia Chikuma

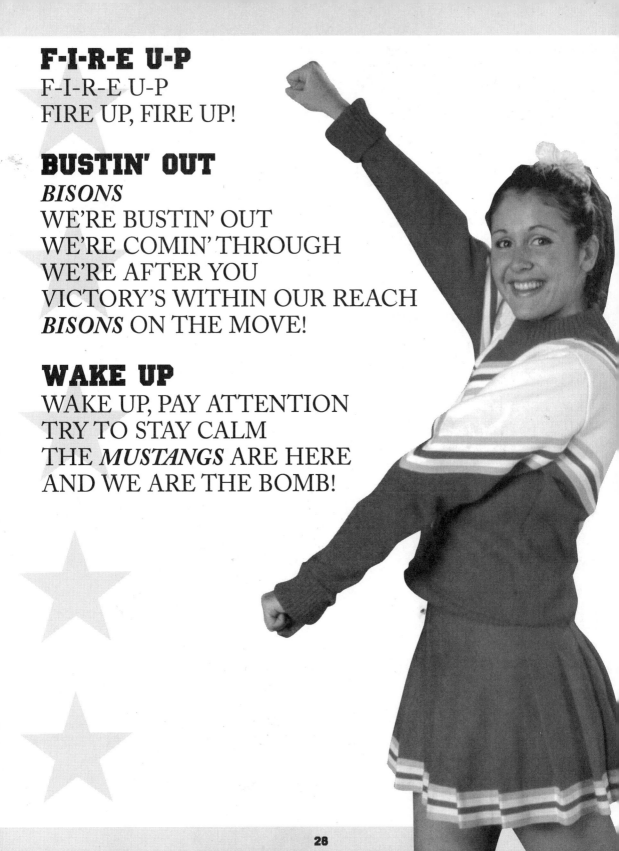

F-I-R-E U-P
F-I-R-E U-P
FIRE UP, FIRE UP!

BUSTIN' OUT
BISONS
WE'RE BUSTIN' OUT
WE'RE COMIN' THROUGH
WE'RE AFTER YOU
VICTORY'S WITHIN OUR REACH
BISONS ON THE MOVE!

WAKE UP
WAKE UP, PAY ATTENTION
TRY TO STAY CALM
THE *MUSTANGS* ARE HERE
AND WE ARE THE BOMB!

TIME

THE TIME IS RIGHT
FOR VICTORY TONIGHT
THE SCOREBOARD WILL SHOW
THAT WE ARE IN THE KNOW
WE KNOW WHAT TO SAY
AND WE KNOW HOW TO PLAY
THAT'S WHY THE TIME IS RIGHT
FOR VICTORY TONIGHT!

JUST BEGINNING

WE ARE JUST BEGINNING
WE ARE JUST BEGINNING
WE ARE JUST BEGINNING TO WHAT?
TO JAM!

GO GO GO

GO, GO, GO
GO YOU MIGHTY *BOBCATS*
FIGHT, FIGHT, FIGHT
FIGHT YOU MIGHTY *BOBCATS*
WIN, WIN, WIN
WIN YOU MIGHTY *BOBCATS*
GO, GO, GO, FIGHT, FIGHT, FIGHT, WIN!
YEAH!

KNOCK YOU OUT

THE *TITANS* ARE THE BEST
AND WE'LL PUT YOU TO THE TEST
WE'RE NUMBER ONE, NO DOUBT
AND WE'LL KNOCK YOU OUT!

FIRED UP AND READY

WE'RE FIRED UP AND READY
OUR TEAM IS ALIVE
SO LET'S GO, GO
SO LET'S FIGHT, FIGHT
WE'VE GOT THE POWER TO BEAT 'EM
    TONIGHT!

SHOUT AND SCREAM GO TEAM

SHOUT, SHOUT EVERYBODY
SCREAM, SCREAM EVERYBODY
EVERYBODY SHOUT, EVERYBODY SCREAM
SHOUT, SCREAM FOR YOUR TEAM!

B-E A-G-G-R-E-S-S-I-V-E

B-E A-G-G-R-E-S-S-I-V-E
BE AGGRESSIVE, *DOLPHINS* BE AGGRESSIVE!

S-C-O-R-E

S-C-O-R-E
SCORE *RAMBLERS*, LET'S SCORE!

LET'S GO

LET'S GO, LET'S GO, LET'S REALLY GO
LET'S FIGHT, LET'S FIGHT,
    LET'S REALLY FIGHT
LET'S WIN, LET'S WIN, LET'S WIN, TONIGHT
LET'S GO, FIGHT, WIN
TONIGHT!

IF YOU CAN'T JAM WITH US

IF YOU CAN'T JAM WITH US
THEN YOU CAN'T JAM AT ALL!

NO DOUBT

NO DOUBT ABOUT IT
STAND UP AND SHOUT IT
THE *STARS* ARE
        NUMBER ONE!

"Stunting is the best. It makes your cheers look ten times better. Make sure that you take it seriously and stay safe."
—Tamara Diles

ENTERPRISE

READY 👏 ENTERPRISE
ORIOLES
WE'LL SET YOU ON FIRE
RIGHT FROM THE START
WE'VE GOT 👏
WHAT NO ONE ELSE HAS GOT 👏
THE *ORIOLES* ARE SCORCHING HOT! 👏 👏 👏

FUTURE

THE FUTURE, THE FUTURE
YES WE CAN PREDICT THE FUTURE
WE CAN LOOK AHEAD IN TIME
AND WHAT DO WE SEE?
THE POINTS
ARE RISING
OUR TEAM IS OUT THERE JIVING
WE'RE GOING TO GO
WE'RE GOING TO FIGHT
WE'RE GOING TO WIN THIS GAME TONIGHT!

H-E-L-L-O

H-E-L-L-O FROM *GHS*,
BULLDOGS, WE WISH YOU LUCK,
     FROM . . . [roll call]
LET'S GO
TIGERS LET'S DO IT
YOU'VE GOT THE STUFF TO PROVE IT
FIRE UP TO WIN
TIGERS 👏 👏
DO IT AGAIN!

GO FOR THE WIN

GO *HORNETS*, GO FOR THE WIN
FIGHT *HORNETS*, FIGHT TILL THE END
WIN *HORNETS*, YOU KNOW IT CAN BE DONE
BECAUSE WE ARE THE *HORNETS*,
     NUMBER ONE!

SUCCESS

S-U-C-C-E-S-S
THAT'S THE WAY WE SPELL SUCCESS!
SUCCESS!

INTO THE GROOVE

GET INTO THE GROOVE
SHOW 'EM HOW TO MOVE
GET INTO THE SWING
SHOW 'EM WHO IS KING
WIN THIS GAME TONIGHT
SHOW 'EM HOW TO FIGHT!

S-T-E-A-L

S-T-E-A-L
STEAL THAT BALL!

BIG G, LITTLE O

BIG "G," LITTLE "O"
GO! GO!

WE LIKE IT

TAKE IT AWAY
TAKE IT AWAY
WE LIKE IT!
WE LIKE IT!

TAKE IT TO THE TOP
TAKE IT TO THE TOP
NO WE WILL NEVER STOP
WE'RE THE HOTTEST THING AROUND
WE'RE THE BADDEST THING IN TOWN
SO WATCH OUT FOR THIS TEAM
'CAUSE WE ARE FOLLOWING OUR DREAM
TAKE IT
TAKE IT
TAKE IT TO THE TOP
WE CAN'T
WE CAN'T
WE JUST CAN'T BE STOPPED!

WIN IT
OH, WE'RE GONNA WIN IT
I SAY, WE'RE GONNA WIN IT
OH, WE'RE GONNA WIN IT
I SAY, WE'RE GONNA WIN IT!

ELECTRIFIED
ELECTRIFIED LET'S HEAR IT
HIGH-POWERED SPIRIT!

"Cheering is such a good experience. You make so many good friends. The games are all so much fun. I love it."
—Kasi Jones

WATCH THAT BALL

WATCH THAT BALL
WATCH IT MOVE
TONIGHT WE WILL PROVE
THAT WE CAN HAVE IT ALL
IF WE JUST WATCH THAT BALL!

PSYCHED TONIGHT

HEY *REBELS*, WE'RE PSYCHED TONIGHT!
WE'RE FIRED UP AND PREPARED TO FIGHT!
LOOK OUT VIKINGS WE'RE READY TO PLAY!
NUMBER ONE WE'LL BE, WE'RE ON OUR WAY!

DON'T MESS

DON'T MESS! DON'T MESS!
DON'T MESS WITH THE BEST, 'CAUSE THE
    BEST DON'T MESS
DON'T FOOL! DON'T FOOL!
DON'T FOOL WITH THE COOL, 'CAUSE THE
    COOL DON'T FOOL.
FROM EAST
TO WEST
WE ARE THE BEST
GO *GREYHOUNDS*!

GET IT TOGETHER AND GO

GET IT TOGETHER AND GO YOU *DOLPHINS*!
GET IT TOGETHER AND GO!

STRAWBERRY SHORTCAKE

STRAWBERRY SHORTCAKE
HUCKLEBERRY PIE
TAKE THAT VICTORY
TO THE SKY!

STAND CLEAR

THE *GIANTS* TEAM IS HERE, HEY
THIS IS OUR YEAR
WE'RE BACK, STAND CLEAR
LET'S DO IT AGAIN: GO, FIGHT, WIN!

THINK FAST

TAKE 'EM FOR A RIDE
TAKE THIS THING IN STRIDE
THINK FAST
THINK FAST
AND WE WILL HAVE A BLAST
DON'T WAIT
DON'T WAIT
PUT YOUR HEADS TOGETHER
    AND GET THIS STRAIGHT!

SUPER DUPER

S-U-P-E-R
SUPER DUPER THAT'S WHAT WE ARE
G-R-E-A-T
SUPER GREAT THAT'S WHAT WE'LL BE
GO *BEARS!*

HYPNOTIZE

SAY 1, 2, 3, 4, 5,
COMETS GONNA HYPNOTIZE
SAY 6, 7, 8, 9, 10,
LET'S ROUND IT UP AND DO IT AGAIN
SAY 10, 9, 8, 7, 6,
COMETS GIRLS DON'T PLAY NO TRICKS
SAY 5, 4, 3, 2, 1,
DON'T GO YET 'CAUSE WE AIN'T DONE
WE KNOW WINNING IS OUR PLAN
COMETS GIRLS LET'S
    CLAP OUR HANDS 👏 👏 👏
GIRLS THIS BEAT SOUNDS INCOMPLETE
COMETS GIRLS LET'S
    STAMP OUR FEET 👞 👞 👞 👞 👞
STOP!

UNITED

UNITED, WE ARE
UNITED, WE'LL BE
'CAUSE WE'RE THE *THUNDERCATS*,
WE'RE OUT FOR
VICTORY!
YEAH!

ON THE LOOSE

THE *WOLVES* ARE ON THE LOOSE
HEY FANS, PUMP UP THE JUICE!

WON'T TAKE DEFEAT

WE'VE GOT A TEAM
THAT CAN'T BE BEAT
WE NEVER SAY
THE WORD DEFEAT
WE CAN'T BE BEAT
WON'T TAKE DEFEAT
WE CAN'T BE BEAT
WON'T TAKE DEFEAT, UH-HUH
YOU KNOW WE GOT THE SPIRIT,
THE MIGHT,
'CAUSE WE'RE GONNA WIN
THIS GAME TONIGHT
SO LET'S FIGHT!

BREAK AWAY

BREAK AWAY
MOVE AHEAD
GET TOUGH TODAY AND PLAY
I'M READY TO HEAR YOU SAY
WE'RE BREAKING AWAY
BREAK AWAY!

DEFENSE

DEFENSE *TIGERS*
PUSH THAT TEAM ASIDE
LET'S MAKE THEM RUN AND HIDE!
GET IN GEAR AND GO TEAM
TAKE THE WINNING STRIDE!

WHO'S GONNA WIN THIS
THE TEAM WAS IN A HUDDLE
THE CAPTAIN AT THE HEAD
SHE STOOD UP AND SHOUTED
AND THIS IS WHAT SHE SAID
WHO'S GONNA WIN THIS
WHO'S GONNA WIN THIS
WHO'S GONNA WIN THIS NOW?
WE'RE GONNA WIN THIS
WE'RE GONNA WIN THIS
WE'RE GONNA WIN THIS NOW!

STEP TO THE BACK
STEP TO THE BACK
GET OUT OF OUR WAY
WE ARE THE *BULLS*,
AND WE'LL BLOW YOU AWAY!

GOTTA GET TOUGH
GOTTA GET TOUGH
GOTTA GET TOUGH GO
LET'S GET TO IT COME ON GUYS YOU CAN
    DO IT
GO GO FIGHT FIGHT
GOTTA GONNA WIN
TONIGHT!

EXTRA EXTRA

EXTRA EXTRA READ ALL ABOUT IT
WE GOT THE TEAM
THERE'S NO DOUBT ABOUT IT
TO THE EAST TO THE WEST
TO THE EAST TO THE WEST
TURN AROUND TOUCH THE GROUND
CLAP HIGH 👏 CLAP LOW 👏
   CLAP HIGH 👏 CLAP LOW 👏
TURN AROUND TOUCH THE GROUND
LET'S GO!

HEY EVERYBODY

HEY EVEYBODY UP IN THE STANDS
MAKE SOME NOISE AND CLAP YOUR HANDS
GET ON UP OUT OF YOUR SEAT
STOMP YOUR FEET TO THE BEAT 👞 👞 👞 👞
THE *TIGERS* CAN'T BE BEAT!

SCORE BIG

SCORE BIG
SCORE MORE
YES WE'VE GOT SOME IN STORE!
WE'LL RUN
WE'LL FIGHT
WE'LL SURPRISE YOU ALL TONIGHT!
WE KNOW HOW TO PLAY THIS GAME
AND WE'LL MAKE YOU REMEMBER OUR
   NAME!

A LITTLE LOUDER
WE ARE THE *DOLPHINS*
WE COULDN'T BE PROUDER
AND IF YOU CAN'T HEAR
WE'LL SHOUT A LITTLE LOUDER!

WHIP IT
W-H-I-P WHIP IT TO A VICTORY, WHIP IT, WOO!
   AND WHIP IT GOOD! 👏 👏 👏

STAND UP AND CHEER
GRIZZLY FANS, GET READY
THIS IS OUR YEAR
THE TIME IS NOW
WE'LL SHOW YOU HOW
STAND UP AND CHEER!

D-E-F-E-N-S-E
D-E
F-E
N-S-E
DEFENSE *LIONS!* DEFENSE!

"Some of the best times I've had have been on my cheer squad. I've made great friends. I know I will look back and smile when I think about my years on the squad."

—Brooke Barrus

POWER

BOBCATS OH YES!
WE'VE GOT THE POWER
WE'VE GOT THE STRENGTH
WE ARE THE BEST
WE'LL OVERCOME THE REST
POWER WE'VE GOT HOT!
POWER WE'VE GOT HOT!

FOOTBALL CHEERS

YOU MIGHT BE GOOD

YOU MIGHT BE GOOD AT BASKETBALL,
YOU MIGHT BE GOOD AT TRACK
BUT WHEN IT COMES TO FOOTBALL
YOU MIGHT AS WELL STEP BACK!
GO *JAGUARS* GO!
GO *JAGUARS* GO!
GO *JAGUARS!* GO *JAGUARS!* GO *JAGUARS!*
GO!

FIRST AND TEN

FIRST AND TEN!
FIRST DOWN, DO IT AGAIN!

TOUCHDOWN

TOUCHDOWN *WILDCATS!*
SCORE! SCORE!

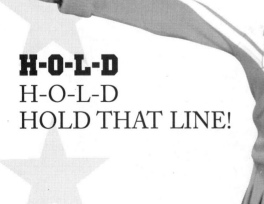

H-O-L-D

H-O-L-D
HOLD THAT LINE!

IT'S TIME

NOW IT'S TIME TO TIGHTEN THAT LINE
HOLD 'EM DEFENSE, HOLD 'EM!

SACK THAT QUARTERBACK

SACK THAT QUARTERBACK
CRASH THROUGH THAT LINE!

GOAL

TOUCHDOWN *FALCONS*,
   TAKE IT TO THAT GOAL
EVERYBODY YELL SCORE (SCORE!)
TOUCHDOWN 👏, SIX MORE!

WE WANT A T-D

WE WANT A T-D 👏 👏 👏
WHAT'S THAT? A TOUCHDOWN!

"Cheerleaders promote spirit throughout the community and represent their schools in a positive way. Always keep a good attitude, keep smiling, and enjoy what you are doing, because cheer is the best sport around."
—Sarah Short

OUTER SPACE

IF YOU THROW THAT BALL INTO
    OUTER SPACE
IT MIGHT JUST LAND IN THE RIGHT PLACE
IF YOU THROW THAT BALL FAR ACROSS
    THE FIELD
VICTORY WILL SURELY BE SEALED!

BASKETBALL CHEERS

FLY

LET'S FLY! LET'S FLY!
LET'S MOVE SO FAST WE CAN FLY!
YOU CAN JUMP SO HIGH THAT THE SKY
COMES DOWN
WHEN YOU LAND ON THE GROUND
WHEN YOU SOAR
YOU CAN SCORE
YOUR HANDS
ON THE BALL
YOUR EYES ON TOP OF IT ALL
YOU CAN SEE THE BASKET STRAIGHT AHEAD
NOTHING CAN STOP YOU AND LIKE I SAID
LET'S FLY!

BASKET BASKET

BASKET BASKET
WE WANT TWO!
GET THAT BALL
TAKE IT AWAY
WE WANT TWO!

DOWN THE FLOOR

DOWN DOWN DOWN THE FLOOR
UP UP UP THE SCORE
DOWN THE FLOOR
UP THE SCORE
TWO POINTS MORE!

SINK IT

SINK IT
PUT IT THROUGH
COME ON *HUSKIES*
SHOOT TWO!

ONE, TWO, THREE, FOUR

ONE, TWO, THREE, FOUR
WHAT DO YOU THINK THAT HOOP IS FOR?
SINK IT *BLUEJAYS* SINK IT
SINK IT *BLUEJAYS* SINK IT!

SENSATION

ALL ACROSS THE NATION
THERE'S A BASKETBALL SENSATION
THAT MAKES YOU WANT TO SLIDE
AND MOVE FROM SIDE TO SIDE
COME ON, LET'S ROCK
COME ON, LET'S ROLL
LET'S BOOGIE ON DOWN TO THE OTHER SIDE
    OF TOWN
LET'S TURN THIS GAME UPSIDE DOWN!

YOU TRAVELED

YOU TRAVELED
YOU WALKED
YOU TOOK TOO MANY STEPS
THE NEXT TIME YOU TRAVEL
TAKE THE B-U-S!

FIRED UP

WE'RE FIRED UP, WE'RE SIZZLIN'
WE'RE TURNING UP THE HEAT
'CAUSE WHEN IT COMES TO BASKETBALL
THE *WILDCATS* CAN'T BE BEAT!

STEP UP TO THE LINE

STEP UP TO THE LINE
LOOKIN' MIGHTY FINE
HEY, HEY THROUGH THE HOOP
SHOOT IT! SINK IT! SCORE!

HOOP, HOOP

DRIBBLE IT
SHOOT, SHOOT,
TAKE THAT BALL TO THE
HOOP, HOOP!

GRAB THAT BALL

GRAB THAT BALL
BRING IT DOWN
GRAB THAT BALL
REBOUND!

UP IN THE AIR

UP IN THE AIR
OVER THE RIM
COME ON *KNIGHTS*
PUT IT IN!

SLAM IT

SLAM IT
JAM IT
GET THAT BALL
AND SCORE TWO POINTS
SLAM IT
JAM IT
PUT IT THROUGH
FOR TWO!

DRIBBLE IT, PASS IT

DRIBBLE IT, PASS IT,
WE WANT A BASKET!

REBOUND

R-E
R-E-B
R-E-B-O-U-N-D
REBOUND
REBOUND!

HIT THE SKY

IF YOU JUMP REAL HIGH
YOU CAN HIT THE SKY
YOU CAN TOUCH THE CLOUDS
YOU CAN MAKE US PROUD
PUT THE BALL IN THE BASKET NOW
WE'LL SCORE ONCE MORE, WE'LL SHOW
    THEM HOW!

WISH
COME ON *BLAZERS*
GRANT OUR WISH
ALL WE WANNA HEAR IS
SWISH!

THE OTHER WAY
WE WANT THAT BALL TO
    GO THE OTHER WAY
GRAB IT, STEAL IT, TAKE IT AWAY!

YOU FOULED!
YOU FOULED
YOU FOULED
YOU TOUCH TOO MUCH
YOU FOULED!

STEAL IT
STEAL IT
SWIPE IT
ANY WAY YOU LIKE IT
GET THAT BALL!

DON'T FORGET
DON'T FORGET
TO PUT IT IN THE NET
DON'T LET US DOWN
PASS THAT BALL AROUND!

"It's so much fun to cheer at games and perform in front of big crowds. But it takes a lot of dedication and hard work to survive practices. Remember, practice makes perfect."
—Julia Burwell

SOCCER CHEERS

SOCCER

S-O DOUBLE C-E-R SOCCER YELL GO
    (GO!)
S-O DOUBLE C-E-R SOCCER YELL FIGHT
    (FIGHT!)
S-O DOUBLE C-E-R SOCCER YELL WIN
    (WIN!)
S-O DOUBLE C-E-R GO, FIGHT, WIN
YELL IT
    (GO, FIGHT, WIN!)

K-I-C-K

K-I-C-K
BLOCK THAT KICK!

MOVE IT

MOVE IT
DOWN THE FIELD
SCORE! SCORE!

CROWD CHEERS

GOT THE BEAT

THE *SPARTANS* HAVE GOT THE BEAT,
WHAT WE SAY YOU REPEAT
GO (GO!)
GO! GO! (GO! GO!)
GO FOR IT (GO FOR IT!)
SPARTAN TEAM, GO FOR IT
    (*SPARTAN* TEAM, GO FOR IT!)

WHISPER

COME ON CROWD
LET'S HEAR YOU WHISPER
GOPHERS (*GOPHERS!*)
COME ON CROWD
LET'S HEAR YOU SAY IT
GOPHERS (*GOPHERS!*)
COME ON CROWD
LET'S HEAR YOU YELL IT
GOPHERS (*GOPHERS!*)

ONE! WE ARE THE BULLDOGS

ONE! WE ARE THE *BULLDOGS!*
TWO! A LITTLE BIT LOUDER!
THREE! I STILL CAN'T HEAR YOU!
FOUR! MORE! MORE! MORE!

ONE, TWO, THREE

ROCKETS FANS ON THE LEFT YELL GO!
ONE, TWO, THREE (GO!)
ROCKETS ON THE RIGHT YELL FIGHT
ONE, TWO, THREE (FIGHT!)
LEFT (GO! GO!)
RIGHT (FIGHT! FIGHT!)
STAND TOGETHER UNITE ALL RIGHT!
TOGETHER AGAIN YOU SAY GO, FIGHT, WIN!
    (GO, FIGHT, WIN!)

I SAY VICIOUS

WHEN I SAY VICIOUS YOU SAY *VIKINGS*
VISCIOUS (*VIKINGS!*) VICIOUS (*VIKINGS)*
WHEN I SAY SUPER YOU SAY GREAT
SUPER (GREAT!) SUPER (GREAT!)
WHEN I SAY NUMBER YOU SAY ONE
NUMBER (ONE!) NUMBER (ONE!)

HEY FANS

HEY FANS IN THE STANDS YELL GO (GO!)
LOUDER NOW WE'LL SHOW YOU HOW
YELL FIGHT (FIGHT!)
PUT IT ALL TOGETHER
YELL GO, FIGHT, WIN
(GO, FIGHT, WIN!)

PULL TOGETHER

CHARGERS FANS KNOW WHAT TO DO
PULL TOGETHER FOR YOU KNOW WHO
YELL LET'S GO *CHARGERS*
(LET'S GO *CHARGERS!*)
LET'S GO *CHARGERS*
(LET'S GO *CHARGERS!*)

HOLD TIGHT

WITH ALL YOUR MIGHT
JETS HOLD TIGHT
SHAKE 'EM UP
SHAKE 'EM DOWN
PUSH THAT OFFENSE ALL AROUND
JETS MAKE IT OVER THE LINE
ONE MORE TIME
COME ON CROWD
JOIN RIGHT IN
GO *JETS* GO
(GO *JETS* GO!)

IF YOU WANT TO WIN

IF YOU WANT TO WIN
YOU'VE GOT TO CHEER WITH ALL YOUR
      MIGHT
WHEN I SAY GO, YOU SAY FIGHT
GO (FIGHT!)
GO (FIGHT!)
GO, GO (FIGHT, FIGHT!)
GO, FIGHT, WIN!

BEAT 'EM!

B (*TIGERS*)
E (*TIGERS*)
A (*TIGERS*)
T (*TIGERS*)
B (*TIGERS*)
E (*TIGERS*)
A (*TIGERS*)
T (*TIGERS*)
B-E-A-T
BEAT 'EM *TIGERS*, BEAT 'EM *TIGERS*
BEAT 'EM!

"Cheer has been an awesome experience for me, and I have met a lot of neat people. I have learned that you are a major role model for your school. Just have fun!"
—Heidi Isaacson

WHO'S GONNA WIN?

WHO'S GONNA WIN THIS GAME TONIGHT?
(WE ARE, WE ARE, WE ARE!)
WHO'S GONNA WIN THIS GAME TONIGHT?
(WE ARE, WE ARE, WE ARE!)

WE ARE THE . . .

WE ARE THE *PIRATES*, THE MIGHTY MIGHTY
    PIRATES
EVERYWHERE WE GO, PEOPLE WANT TO
    KNOW WHO WE ARE
SO WE TELL 'EM, WE ARE THE *PIRATES*
HEY, HEY IT'S TIME TO FIGHT
EVERYBODY YELL *GREEN AND WHITE*
(*GREEN AND WHITE!*)
HEY, HEY LET'S DO IT AGAIN
EVERYBODY YELL GO, FIGHT, WIN
(GO, FIGHT, WIN!)

STAND UP

STAND UP, BE PROUD
SAY YOUR NAME OUT LOUD
WE ARE THE *DOLPHINS*
(WE ARE THE *DOLPHINS!*)
THE MIGHTY *DOLPHINS*
GO (GO!)
GO (GO!)

"The best cheerleader is one who has spirit, along with a positive attitude. Cheer is hard work, so don't let anyone ever tell you it's not a sport."

—Lea Lo

WE'VE GOT SOME SPIRIT

HEY, WE'VE GOT SOME SPIRIT! GO, GO, GO!
HEY, WE'VE GOT SOME SPIRIT! 👏
ME AND MY FRIENDS LIKE TO CHEER AT
    GAMES
SOME CALL IT YELLIN' BUT IT'S ALL THE
    SAME!
WE ALWAYS STAND UP AND CHEER FOR OUR
    TEAM
SO COME ON EVERYBODY, LET ME HEAR YOU
    SCREAM!
HEY, WE'VE GOT SOME SPIRIT! GO, GO, GO!
HEY, WE'VE GOT SOME SPIRIT! 👏

STAND UP AND CLAP

TROJANS FANS UP IN THE STANDS
STAND UP AND CLAP 👏 👏 👏
    YOUR 👏 👏 👏
    HANDS 👏 👏 👏 👏 GO BIG BLUE!
CLAP 👏 👏 👏
    YOUR 👏 👏 👏
    HANDS 👏 👏 👏
    GO BIG BLUE!
NOW STOMP 👞 👞 👞 YOUR 👞 👞 👞 FEET
    👞 👞 👞 GO BIG BLUE!

TWO TIMES FOUR

TWO TIMES FOUR IS HALF OF SIXTEEN 👏
ALL FOR THE *WOLVES* 👏 A-LEAN, LEAN
A-LEAN A-LEAN A-LEAN A-LEAN 👏
    A-LEAN LEAN 👏
A-LEAN A-LEAN A-LEAN A-LEAN 👏
    A-LEAN LEAN 👏
TWO TIMES SIX IS HALF OF TWENTY-FOUR 👏
ALL FOR THE BOBCATS 👏 A-BACK-FORWARD
A-BACK A-BACK A-BACK A-BACK 👏
    A-FORWARD FORWARD
A-BACK A-BACK A-BACK A-BACK 👏
    A-FORWARD FORWARD!